Napoleon's
Oracle

NAPOLEON'S ORACLE

THE ANCIENT BOOK OF FATE FROM EGYPT'S VALLEY OF THE KINGS

INTRODUCTION BY JUDY HALL

CICO BOOKS

London

First published in 2003 by Cico Books Ltd

32 Great Sutton Street London EC1V 0NB

This edition copyright © Cico Books 2003

The right of Judy Hall to be identified as author of the introduction
to this text has been asserted by her in accordance with the
Copyright, Designs and Patents Act of 1988.

10 9 8 7 6 5 4 3 2 1

A CIP catalogue record for this book is available from the British Library

ISBN 1 903116 59 7

Design: David Fordham

Printed and bound in Singapore

Judy Hall is an international author, astrologer, psychic, healer and broadcaster.
She has written twenty books and her work has been translated into
twelve languages. She is a tutor with the London School of Astrology
and the College of Psychic Studies in London.
A trained healer and counsellor, she has been a psychic all her life
and has a wide experience of many systems of divination and natural healing methods.
Judy has a B.Ed in religious studies and an extensive knowledge
of world religions and mythology.

CONTENTS

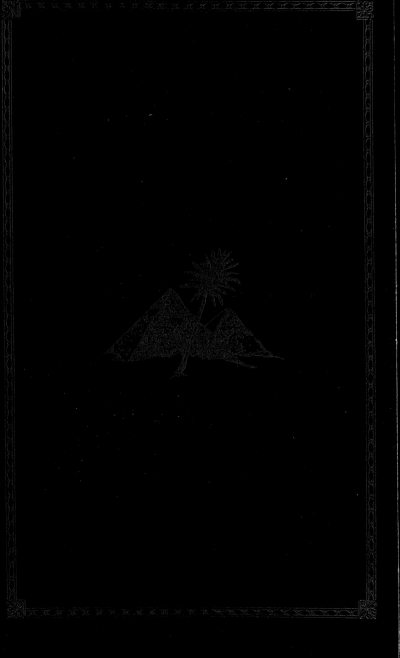

INTRODUCTION

In 1975 I HAD THE GOOD FORTUNE to meet the metaphysician and Western Mystery Tradition priestess, the late Christine Hartley, who became my mentor. Christine had worked closely with Dion Fortune and her magical colleagues. Shortly after our first meeting, Christine handed me a pile of tattered, handwritten pages headed "The Oraculum". She told me that it was an esoteric secret, passed down through the ages, which had come into the possession of the Emperor Napoleon and his wife Josephine, and had been made public after his death.

Despite its unprepossessing appearance, the Oraculum was uncannily accurate. I used it for many years until it was inadvertently lost in a house move. Shortly afterwards, a friend gave me an old, much thumbed, copy of *Napoleon's Book of Fate* which she had found in a second-hand book store. To my delight, it contained the Oraculum, which I still use to this day and which is reproduced in this facsimile edition.

This Oracle is as accurate now as it would have been five thousand years ago, which is why it has been continuously in print for the last two hundred years. The questions are universal, encompassing all cultures and ages. Its language has been updated in this new twenty- first century edition to make it more accessible to people who now need guidance as to what the future holds.

HISTORY OF THE ORACLE

A RENAISSANCE OF EGYPTIAN and other divination methods swept through Europe in the early nineteenth century. This was the first time that formerly secret teachings were made available to the mass market and publication of works such as the Oraculum, also known as *The Book of Fate,* was an immediate success. As H. Kirchenhoffer, one of the earliest translators from the German, put it: "the Book of Fate, in its English dress, is adapted to all conditions of life, and persons of every rank and capacity will now have an opportunity of consulting it, and of regulating their future conduct according to its Oracular Councils."

As befits something of such deep esoteric and occult significance, the origins of the Oraculum and how it came to be made public are shrouded in mystery. They are somewhat obscured by different versions of events. All sources agree that the Oraculum itself was found as a papyrus scroll in an Egyptian tomb following the French invasion of Egypt in 1798-1799. When Napoleon, then a General, addressed his troops at the Great Pyramid at Giza on 21 July 1798 he told them: "Soldiers, from the height of these pyramids, forty centuries look down on you." He was determined to explore that history.

At the time, little was known in the West of this archaic civilization apart from what classical writers and one or two eighteenth-century travellers had reported. It fascinated Napoleon. The military expedition was accompanied by 167 scholars, including three astronomers and eight draughtsmen, who recorded the journey in great detail. These scholars became the Institute of Egypt and it was they who found the Rosetta Stone that enabled hieroglyphs to be translated. Napoleon's archaeologists amassed many thousands of objects. Purportedly, among the antiquities that they discovered was the Oraculum.

According to one source, published in 1822, it was found by M. Sonnini in a royal tomb in the Valley of the Kings near Thebes (modern Luxor) attached to the breast of a well-preserved, and most beautiful, mummy. Napoleon immediately consulted a Coptic priest who was able to translate the hieroglyphs. For secrecy, they were dictated to Napoleon's secretary who transcribed them into German. Neither the papyrus nor the translation were made public at the time.

The Oracle became one of Napoleon's most prized possessions. It travelled with him everywhere. It is said that Napoleon relied upon the Oracle for many years, and yet rejected its counsel when his pride and ambition became overwhelming, which led to his downfall. In one version of events, passed on through esoteric tradition via Christine Hartley, the Oracle travelled into exile at St Helena with Napoleon and was apparently removed from Napoleon's death-bed by a "companion in exile" – and possible murderer – who sold it as part of a bundle of the Emperor's most private possessions on the streets of Jamestown from where it travelled, in the hands of an unknown collector, to Paris.

However, there is another version of events which says that the cabinet in which Napoleon kept the Oracle was amongst possessions of necessity discarded on the battlefield after the disastrous Battle of Leipzig in 1815. According to H. Kirchenhoffer, who published a translation of *The Book of Fate* in 1822, Napoleon risked his life trying to rescue the Oracle but failed. It was found by a Prussian officer who sold it to a French general, a prisoner of war in the fortress of Koningsburg. The general, recognising it as a possession of the Emperor from the coat of arms emblazoned on the cabinet, intended to take it back to France. Unfortunately he died following amputation of his right arm before he could accomplish this. In his will, the officer enjoined his family to put the manuscript into Napoleon's own hands, but this proved impossible.

Whilst Napoleon was in exile, it was conveyed to his second wife, the Empress Marie Louise. Following the Emperor's death in 1821, H. Kirchenhoffer claims it was handed to him for translation. The 1822 edition of *The Book of Fate Formerly in the Possession of and Used By Napoleon*, published in London on June 1st, was dedicated to "Her Imperial Highness, the ex-Empress of France". According to H. Kirchenhoffer, the German manuscript had notations in the Emperor's own hand of questions on which he had consulted the Oracle. In answer to the question: "Will my name be immortalized and will posterity

applaud it?" the answer was given: "Thy name will be handed down, with the memory of thy deeds, to the most distant posterity." A most prophetic reply and an excellent way of establishing provenance.

Provenance is important to a metaphysician because "direct transmission" is considered to be the most powerful, and empowering, form of knowledge. By accessing an ancient Egyptian oracle which has come straight from the tomb of its former owner, Napoleon was tapping into the magical powers of that arcane civilization.

The Kirchenhoffer version shows the Oracle in its 32-question form accompanied by an introductory account of the importance of oracles in the ancient world, together with a treatise known as The Writing of Balapsis by Command of Hermes Trismegistus unto the Priests of the Great Temple. In this treatise, the priests are exhorted to take strict charge of the Oracle, letting no one but priests touch it. They are instructed to place a copy at the left breast of Pharaohs and High Priests after mummification. In including this, Kirchenhoffer may well have been trying to strengthen the provenance of the Oracle and to rebut those who might accuse him of forgery.

A somewhat different version of the oracle was first published in Europe in 1835 as Napoleon's Book of Fate and Oraculum. This version contained both a 32- and 16-question Oracle — the answers to these and the Kirchenhoffer edition being virtually the same — with additional material on fortune-telling, palmistry, the meaning of omens and other methods of divination. This present facsimile edition reproduces the deluxe 1890 version of that Oraculum.

AUTHENTICITY

THE QUESTION WILL NO DOUBT BE ASKED: Is the Oracle genuine? Well, according to occult tradition it is. Christine Hartley was convinced it had come from ancient Egypt. There seems little doubt that Napoleon did indeed have such an Oracle and consulted it frequently. If H. Kirchenhoffer is to be believed, the manuscript he translated had the

Emperor's own handwriting upon it. The question to ask is whether this oracle was genuinely from an ancient Egyptian source or whether it was a more modern oracle. The concerns that it addresses would have been as relevant to a Pharaoh of Egypt as to the Emperor of France, or to their subjects, despite suggestions that they are more politically attuned to the French Revolution.

Many artefacts sold to travellers in Egypt were – and are – undoubtedly fakes, but this was long before tourism got underway. It is possible that one of the Emperor's entourage, knowing his interest in such matters, could have purchased a faked oracle and covered up its origins. But M. Sonnini, who allegedly found it, was a much-respected scholar. That he did not include the papyrus in the official record of the expedition can be explained by Napoleon's insistence on secrecy.

It has been suggested that no one at that time would have been able to translate hieroglyphs – the Rosetta Stone taking over twenty years to decipher. However, esoteric knowledge is passed down in secret and the Copts inherited a great deal from their pharaonic forebears. It is certainly possible that the ability to read hieroglyphs was transmitted down through the generations. It was his knowledge of Coptic that helped Champollior decipher the Rosetta Stone. The Coptic liturgy, although written in the Greek script which appears on the Rosetta Stone, is remarkably similar to ancient Egyptian and the two religions overlapped. Coptic priests were the guardians of many esoteric secrets.

The Oraculum has certain similarities to oracles that are known to be ancient, such as the *I Ching*. These methods of divination function rather like a computer. Based on the binary system, it may be no coincidence that the number of possible answers to the Oraculum, 1,024, is the number of bytes in the kilobyte used by modern computer programmers. It is also possible that dominoes developed from the dots produced in obtaining an answer. The knowledge encoded in Egyptian dominoes may have been lost, but they have traditionally been used for fortune telling and their meanings closely relate to the oracular questions. Sets of dominoes have been found in the tombs, and the game of dominoes is extremely popular in Egypt today. It is still played with great enthusiasm in the back streets of Luxor, close to where the papyrus was purportedly found.

FATE AND DESTINY

NAPOLEON HAD AN INTEREST in oracles and prophecy. Coming from Corsica, he believed in both fate and destiny, which, as his father recorded, was "written in the sky." Had he continued to heed the oracle's advice, Napoleon could well have avoided the path that took him into exile and death. He was deeply superstitious and believed that his first wife Josephine brought him luck but ambition forced him to put her aside in favor of a more highly born Empress.

Josephine was a Creole (pure-born French) woman from Martinique, a land where voodoo and the magical arts flourished. Before setting off for France and her first marriage, she had her fortune told. She was assured that she would marry young (she was 15 when she married), be unhappy (she was), be widowed (she was divorced twice) and would later "become more than the Queen of France" (she became its Empress). Josephine herself read the cards and correctly predicted at least one of Napoleon's victories. Both she and Napoleon could well have been natural psychics. Shortly before his death, the Emperor had a vision of Josephine, by then herself dead, coming to meet him.

THE QUESTIONS

AS THE LANGUAGE of the questions and answers in the original Oraculum reflects translation in the early nineteenth century, they have been updated to make them more accessible without losing the authentic flavour of the oracle. So, for example vicissitudes becomes difficulties and calumny, slander.

The 32 questions are specific and yet comprehensive. They relate to the perennial questions of life: love, fortune, career, health and so on.

Spending a few moments quietly formulating your question helps to connect you to the Oracle and to your own intuitive guidance. It also helps you to be precise and clear in your questioning. Ask the question that gets to the core of the situation you wish to understand. Experience has shown that you can substitute a word or two in a question and still receive the guidance you need. You can also ask a question with the same theme, but on a different subject. Choose the question which is closest in meaning to your query. So, for example, if you feel restricted by your current situation, you could ask question 2: "Will the prisoner be released or continue captive?" You may well receive the answer that "the fettered will soon be free." You will then know that the constriction will soon be released and that your life will move forward again.

Behind the surface meaning of the reply there may lie a much deeper understanding of the situation than at first appears. Question 25 asks whether the patient will recover from illness. Illness may occur at a physical, emotional or psychological level. Distress and disease are an underlying part of "illness." When one woman asked question 25, she was surprised to receive the answer "To ensure recovery, the patient's mind must be kept in cheerful mood, by the conversation of those who are most beloved." She thought at first it was a non-answer, irrelevant. When she thought more deeply, she realized that her condition had in fact reflected the difficulties she was experiencing in her relationship. Her partner had withdrawn from her and seemed distant and cold. She assumed he was falling out of love with her. Her symptoms were based on psychosomatic distress. When she spoke to her partner about the situation, she discovered that he himself had been suffering from depression, which had resulted in him withdrawing. Assured that he did in fact still love her, she was able to offer him much appreciated support, and her illness disappeared.

ALTERNATIVES TO THE QUESTIONS

SOME OF THE ORACULAR QUESTIONS are very specific; others can be adapted to cover other situations. Below are the questions to which this applies, with alternative interpretations in italics.

QUESTION 1: Inform me of any or all particulars which relate to the woman I shall marry
How will I recognize the woman I am to marry?
Is there anything I should be aware of about my future wife?
Is there something I do not yet know about my prospective partner?

QUESTION 2: Will the prisoner be released or continue captive?
Will my circumstances change?
Will the restrictions holding me back be lifted?
Will my life move forward soon?
Is there a way round this obstacle?

QUESTION 3: Shall I live to an old age?
Are there any potential problems with my health?
Should I start a pension fund or insurance now?

QUESTION 4: Shall I live to travel far by sea or land, or to reside in foreign climes?
Should I take a long-haul holiday?
Would it be beneficial for me to live abroad?

QUESTION 5: Shall I be involved in litigation, and, if so, shall I gain or lose my cause?
Should I seek compensation?
Will I qualify for a layoff payment?

QUESTION 6: Shall I make or mar my fortune by gambling?
Will I make a profit on this deal?
Is this a good buy?

QUESTION 7: Shall I ever be able to retire from business with a fortune?
Is this the most appropriate pension plan?
Will I be successful in my career?

QUESTION 8: Shall I be eminent and meet with favour in my pursuits?
Will this job enhance my career path?
Do I have helpful friends to call on?

QUESTION 9: Shall I be successful in my present undertaking?
Is this a good move?
What is the best way forward?
Is this a good time to buy a house?

QUESTION 12: Will my name be immortalized and will posterity applaud it?
Will this idea have an impact on the future of humankind?
Is this course of action ethical?
Will my project be successful?

QUESTION 13: Will the friend I most reckon upon prove faithful or treacherous?
Can I rely upon this information?

QUESTION L6: Shall the stranger soon return from abroad?
Will my lover and I be reunited?

QUESTION 28: Shall I ever find a treasure?
Do I have hidden potential?
Will I win the lottery?
Will I find the perfect house?
Will I find the right present?
Will I find the right dress?

QUESTION 3o: Have I any or many enemies? *Are hidden factors working against me? Can I trust this person?*

THE ANSWERS

Although the language of the oracle has been updated for this edition, some of the replies may still seem quaint. Many of them are proverbs – defined in Nuttall's Dictionary as: "a short sentence expressing a well-known truth" and also as "a maxim which is enigmatical." Oracular replies were, traditionally, enigmatic and some may appear, at first glance, to still be so. They are nevertheless relevant, as a little lateral thinking will show. Identify the sentiment of the reply rather than the precise wording. Asking about a suitable career and being told that you may be a merchant but warned "sell not your soul for gain" does not necessarily mean you should become a salesperson. The oracle's advice is that you should do something in which you can become wholeheartedly involved and in which you believe, rather than taking a job which may pay a high salary but which does not accord with your ethics, or one where your employer has the attitude that it owns you body and soul, and which will involve you paying an ultimately unacceptable price. You could decide that selling or trading is the career for you, but rather than promote a product you have little faith in, you may opt for something ethical, of true benefit and value.

Similarly, if you receive the reply that your career should be connected with the plough do not think only of agriculture – unless you are considering organic farming. Look instead at all opportunities to do with food: the growing, packaging, distribution, selling, marketing and advertising. Food preparation might also figure: a chef is also linked to the plough. You could also look at drink – the purveyor of fine wines has roots in agriculture, as does a hotelier or bar worker. Floristry and horticulture are also synonymous with the plough, and you may decide to become a trendy garden designer or a traditional gardener. Be flexible in your interpretation.

Most ancient oracular replies were somewhat vague and were couched in obscure language – cynics would say that this was so that the priests could later claim they had been misinterpreted. *Napoleon's Oracle* is remarkable in the clarity of its advice. As we have seen, some of the answers may at first appear to be obscure but in actual fact point to a much deeper understanding of the situation. There are one or two answers which seem particularly obscure. But these, on closer examination, have an underlying logic.

Being told that if you like cabbage, you should "use the needle" seems an extremely odd reply to receive to a question on what trade or profession you should follow, for instance. It may not be immediately obvious why a liking for cabbage should be a criteria, but the second part of the answer is clear enough. And, as cabbage is an excellent source of vitamins A, B and C, together with essential minerals and amino acids, it may be that a predilection for cabbage foretells sharp eyesight. Scribes and painters in ancient Egypt were, after all, fed a diet rich in this vegetable for that very reason. Cabbage was traditionally used as a remedy for eye complaints. A sacred plant in ancient Egypt, it was believed that if it was eaten in large quantities before imbibing strong drink, cabbage would protect against drunkenness. Having the shakes the next morning would not be conducive to the use of anything sharp, so those who used cabbage to forestall drunkenness and a resultant hangover would, presumably, remain steady of hand. The Romans, who learned some of their medicine from the Egyptians, regarded cabbage as the most effective hangover cure. It is, in fact, an excellent detoxifier, supporting the work of the liver.

Interestingly, in France cabbage was called "the poor man's medicine," believed to be a useful cure-all. When someone is called a cabbage-head in France, it is not the insult that it is in America and Britain. To the French, a cabbage-head is a person of high intelligence. So, if you do like cabbage, you could consider becoming an acupuncturist, engraver, doctor, nurse, professional knitter, embroiderer, d.j. or tattoo artist. Employment in the fashion industry or as a maker of high-quality shoes could be a distinct possibility.

Oracular answers may offer you a timely warning. If you ask whether you will live to a ripe old age and are told to avoid factors that cause premature decay, then looking at your diet and lifestyle would be wise. Similarly, if you ask whether the person you love loves you, and the answer you receive is that he does not mean what he says and his

heart is false, then it would be wise not to pin all your hopes on that person until time has revealed the veracity of the oracle's reply.

Receiving a reply that implies that death is approaching can cause great concern to questioners. However, in the language of oracles, death usually means an ending – of a relationship or situation – rather than an actual physical death. Even when a physical death is implied, it may offer a period of adjustment or preparation before the event. There may be things that need to be said, actions that have to be taken. Nevertheless, the future is not a fixed and rigid event. Receiving a timely warning can enable you to take steps to look after your health, perhaps exploring some unconventional approaches to ensure the continuation of your good health and well being.

How to
Use
the Oracle

HOW TO USE THE ORACLE

CONSULTING THE ORACLE IS EASY. Identifying the question that most closely reflects your query in the questions on pages 26–27 sets the oracular process in motion. Concentrating on the question focuses your mind and awakens your inner guidance, guiding your hand and drawing the answer to you.

Find your question on pages 26–27 and note its number.

Concentrate on your question.

Without counting, make a row of vertical marks (at least twelve) completely at random across the page.

Now make four more rows of vertical marks, one beneath the other.

Count each row. If it contains an odd number of marks, make one large dot beside it. If it contains an even number of marks make two large dots beside it.

Look up the dot pattern in the Key to the Oracle on pages 28–29, then refer to the answers on pages 30–93.

Napoleon's Oracle

Example:

1. Find your question from the table of questions and note its number: here question no. 20 is chosen.

19 After my death, will my CHILDREN be virtuous and happy?

20 Shall I ever recover from my present MISFORTUNES?

21 Does my DREAM portend good luck or misfortune?

2. Concentrate on your question.

3. Without counting, make a row of vertical marks (at least twelve) completely at random across the page.

Make four more lines:

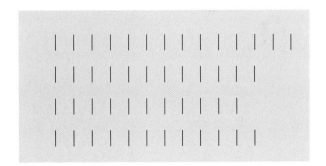

4. THEN LOOK AT EACH LINE AND SEE IF IT CONTAINS AN EVEN

OR ODD NUMBER OF DASHES.

An even number = two dots. Write them like this · ·

An odd number = one dot. Write it like this   ·

WHEN YOU HAVE FINISHED, YOU WILL HAVE FIVE ROWS OF DOTS:

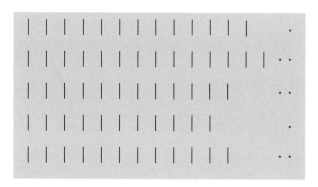

5. LOOK UP YOUR DOT PATTERN AND QUESTION NUMBER IN THE

KEY TO THE ORACLE ON PAGES 28-29. THIS GIVES YOU A LETTER

OF THE ALPHABET OR A SYMBOL.

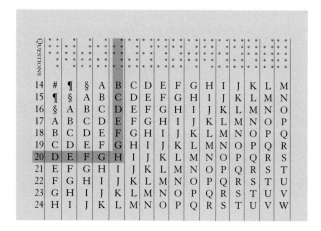

QUESTIONS																
14	#	¶	§	A	B	C	D	E	F	G	H	I	J	K	L	M
15	¶	§	A	B	C	D	E	F	G	H	I	J	K	L	M	N
16	§	A	B	C	D	E	F	G	H	I	J	K	L	M	N	O
17	A	B	C	D	E	F	G	H	I	J	K	L	M	N	O	P
18	B	C	D	E	F	G	H	I	J	K	L	M	N	O	P	Q
19	C	D	E	F	G	H	I	J	K	L	M	N	O	P	Q	R
20	D	E	F	G	H	I	J	K	L	M	N	O	P	Q	R	S
21	E	F	G	H	I	J	K	L	M	N	O	P	Q	R	S	T
22	F	G	H	I	J	K	L	M	N	O	P	Q	R	S	T	U
23	G	H	I	J	K	L	M	N	O	P	Q	R	S	T	U	V
24	H	I	J	K	L	M	N	O	P	Q	R	S	T	U	V	W

6. Look up your dot pattern and letter or symbol in the oracle on pages 30-92. this gives you the answer to your question.

H

::::	By thy marriage thou wilt be envied by others of thy sex.
::::	Be prudent and courteous to all men, and the arrows of slander will be blunted before they reach thee.
::::	It will be thy fate to see many changes.
::::	Thou dreamdest of a wedding which will soon take place.
::::	See that thy misfortunes urge thee not into drunkenness: if so, thou wilt never recover from them.
::::	In the training of thy offspring, let thy discipline be strict, but not severe; lose no opportunity of improving...

The Oracle may well contain a warning as to your future conduct or an obstacle that lies in your path. This is part of an Oracle's function. If you are forewarned, you can act in a way that helps you to manifest a positive future.

The Oracle warns that it is improper for an enquirer to ask two questions on the same day, or even to ask a question with reference to the same subject more than once during a calendar month. In the Kirchenhoffer edition, the writer stresses that questions asked under the light of the moon are likely to be particularly accurate and points out that there are dates on which the Oracle should not be consulted.

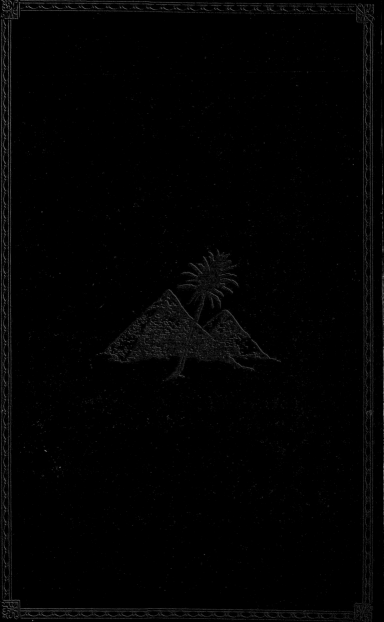

NAPOLEON'S ORACLE

TABLE OF QUESTIONS

1 Inform me of any or of all particulars which relate to
  the woman I shall MARRY?

2 Will the PRISONER be released or continue captive?

3 Shall I live to an OLD AGE?

4 Shall I live to TRAVEL far by sea or land, or to reside in
  foreign climes?

5 Shall I be involved in LITIGATION; and if so, shall I gain or
  lose my cause?

6 Shall I make or mar my fortune by GAMBLING?

7 Shall I ever be able to retire from business with a
  FORTUNE?

8 Shall I be eminent, and meet with FAVOUR
  in my pursuits?

9 Shall I be SUCCESSFUL in my current undertaking?

10 Shall I ever INHERIT PROPERTY?

11 Shall I spend this year HAPPIER than the last?

12 Will my NAME be IMMORTALIZED, and will
   posterity applaud it?

13 Will the FRIEND I most reckon upon prove faithful or
   TREACHEROUS?

14 Will the stolen PROPERTY be RECOVERED, and will the
   THIEF be detected?

15 What is the aspect of the SEASONS, and what POLITICAL
   CHANGES are to take place?

16 Will the STRANGER soon return from abroad?

17 Will my BELOVED prove TRUE in my absence?

18 Will the MARRIAGE about to take place be happy
    and prosperous?

19 After my death, will my CHILDREN be virtuous
    and happy?

20 Shall I ever recover from my present MISFORTUNES?

21 Does my DREAM portend good luck or misfortune?

22 Will it be my lot to experience great DIFFICULTIES
    in this life?

23 Will my reputation be at all or much affected by
    SLANDER?

24 Inform me of all particulars relating to my future
    HUSBAND?

25 Will the PATIENT recover from illness?

26 Does the person whom I LOVE, LOVE and
    regard me?

27 Shall my intended JOURNEY be prosperous or
    unlucky?

28 Shall I ever find a TREASURE?

29 What TRADE or PROFESSION ought I to follow?

30 Have I any, or many ENEMIES?

31 Are ABSENT FRIENDS in good health, and what is
    their present employment?

32 Shall my wife have a SON or a DAUGHTER?

Questions.															
1	A	B	C	D	E	F	G	H	I	J	K	L	M	N	O	P
2	B	C	D	E	F	G	H	I	J	K	L	M	N	O	P	Q
3	C	D	E	F	G	H	I	J	K	L	M	N	O	P	Q	R
4	D	E	F	G	H	I	J	K	L	M	N	O	P	Q	R	S
5	E	F	G	H	I	J	K	L	M	N	O	P	Q	R	S	T
6	F	G	H	I	J	K	L	M	N	O	P	Q	R	S	T	U
7	G	H	I	J	K	L	M	N	O	P	Q	R	S	T	U	V
8	H	I	J	K	L	M	N	O	P	Q	R	S	T	U	V	W
9	I	J	K	L	M	N	O	P	Q	R	S	T	U	V	W	X
10	J	K	L	M	N	O	P	Q	R	S	T	U	V	W	X	Y
11	K	L	M	N	O	P	Q	R	S	T	U	V	W	X	Y	Z
12	L	M	N	O	P	Q	R	S	T	U	V	W	X	Y	Z	*
13	M	N	O	P	Q	R	S	T	U	V	W	X	Y	Z	*	†
14	N	O	P	Q	R	S	T	U	V	W	X	Y	Z	*	†	‡
15	O	P	Q	R	S	T	U	V	W	X	Y	Z	*	†	‡	‖
16	P	Q	R	S	T	U	V	W	X	Y	Z	*	†	‡	‖	¶
17	Q	R	S	T	U	V	W	X	Y	Z	*	†	‡	‖	¶	§
18	R	S	T	U	V	W	X	Y	Z	*	†	‡	‖	¶	§	A
19	S	T	U	V	W	X	Y	Z	*	†	‡	‖	¶	§	A	B
20	T	U	V	W	X	Y	Z	*	†	‡	‖	¶	§	A	B	C
21	U	V	W	X	Y	Z	*	†	‡	‖	¶	§	A	B	C	D
22	V	W	X	Y	Z	*	†	‡	‖	¶	§	A	B	C	D	E
23	W	X	Y	Z	*	†	‡	‖	¶	§	A	B	C	D	E	F
24	X	Y	Z	*	†	‡	‖	¶	§	A	B	C	D	E	F	G
25	Y	Z	*	†	‡	‖	¶	§	A	B	C	D	E	F	G	H
26	Z	*	†	‡	‖	¶	§	A	B	C	D	E	F	G	H	I
27	*	†	‡	‖	¶	§	A	B	C	D	E	F	G	H	I	J
28	†	‡	‖	¶	§	A	B	C	D	E	F	G	H	I	J	K
29	‡	‖	¶	§	A	B	C	D	E	F	G	H	I	J	K	L
30	‖	¶	§	A	B	C	D	E	F	G	H	I	J	K	L	M
31	¶	§	A	B	C	D	E	F	G	H	I	J	K	L	M	N
32	§	A	B	C	D	E	F	G	H	I	J	K	L	M	N	O

KEY TO THE ORACLE

Questions.	** ** ** ** **	* ** ** * **	* ** ** ** **	* ** ** ** **	* ** ** ** **	** * ** ** **	** ** * ** **	** * ** ** **	** ** * ** **	** * ** ** **	** ** * ** **	** * ** ** **	** ** ** * **	** ** ** ** **	* ** ** * **	** ** ** ** **
1	Q	R	S	T	U	V	W	X	Y	Z	*	†	‡	‖	¶	§
2	R	S	T	U	V	W	X	Y	Z	*	†	‡	‖	¶	§	A
3	S	T	U	V	W	X	Y	Z	*	†	‡	‖	¶	§	A	B
4	T	U	V	W	X	Y	Z	*	†	‡	‖	¶	§	A	B	C
5	U	V	W	X	Y	Z	*	†	‡	‖	¶	§	A	B	C	D
6	V	W	X	Y	Z	*	†	‡	‖	¶	§	A	B	C	D	E
7	W	X	Y	Z	*	†	‡	‖	¶	§	A	B	C	D	E	F
8	X	Y	Z	*	†	‡	‖	¶	§	A	B	C	D	E	F	G
9	Y	Z	*	†	‡	‖	¶	§	A	B	C	D	E	F	G	H
10	Z	*	†	‡	‖	¶	§	A	B	C	D	E	F	G	H	I
11	*	†	‡	‖	¶	§	A	B	C	D	E	F	G	H	I	J
12	†	‡	‖	¶	§	A	B	C	D	E	F	G	H	I	J	K
13	‡	‖	¶	§	A	B	C	D	E	F	G	H	I	J	K	L
14	‖	¶	§	A	B	C	D	E	F	G	H	I	J	K	L	M
15	¶	§	A	B	C	D	E	F	G	H	I	J	K	L	M	N
16	§	A	B	C	D	E	F	G	H	I	J	K	L	M	N	O
17	A	B	C	D	E	F	G	H	I	J	K	L	M	N	O	P
18	B	C	D	E	F	G	H	I	J	K	L	M	N	O	P	Q
19	C	D	E	F	G	H	I	J	K	L	M	N	O	P	Q	R
20	D	E	F	G	H	I	J	K	L	M	N	O	P	Q	R	S
21	E	F	G	H	I	J	K	L	M	N	O	P	Q	R	S	T
22	F	G	H	I	J	K	L	M	N	O	P	Q	R	S	T	U
23	G	H	I	J	K	L	M	N	O	P	Q	R	S	T	U	V
24	H	I	J	K	L	M	N	O	P	Q	R	S	T	U	V	W
25	I	J	K	L	M	N	O	P	Q	R	S	T	U	V	W	X
26	J	K	L	M	N	O	P	Q	R	S	T	U	V	W	X	Y
27	K	L	M	N	O	P	Q	R	S	T	U	V	W	X	Y	Z
28	L	M	N	O	P	Q	R	S	T	U	V	W	X	Y	Z	*
29	M	N	O	P	Q	R	S	T	U	V	W	X	Y	Z	*	†
30	N	O	P	Q	R	S	T	U	V	W	X	Y	Z	*	†	‡
31	O	P	Q	R	S	T	U	V	W	X	Y	Z	*	†	‡	‖
32	P	Q	R	S	T	U	V	W	X	Y	Z	*	†	‡	‖	¶

A

As the glorious sun eclipseth the light of the stars, so will the partner of thy bed be accounted the fairest among women.

She will have sons and daughters.

Thy friend is in good health: his thoughts are at present bent on thee.

Though hast no enemies who can in any degree injure thee.

Choose that for which thy genius is the best adapted.

Set not thy mind on searching after that which hath been hidden; but attend diligently to the duties of thy calling.

Choose right trusty companions for thy intended journey, and no ill can befall thee.

Despair not, thy love will meet its due return.

Take not the advice of ignorant pretenders to the art of healing, but apply at once to the fountain head of knowledge.

Thy husband will follow arms.

Look out for the approbation of the virtuous, and heed not the evil report of the wicked.

Oh man! be prepared for any change of fortune which may happen.

It signifieth a speedy marriage.

Though fortune now turn her back upon thee, thine own exertions will soon enable thee to triumph over her capricious humour.

Bestow careful culture on the sapling, and when the tree arriveth at maturity it will produce good fruit.

Let not busy and meddling persons, who call themselves friends, disturb the happiness of the married pair.

A

Take heed that thou givest no just cause for thy beloved to prove inconstant to thee.

No impediment will be thrown in the way of the stranger's quick return.

The scepter of power will be wrested from the conqueror.

The recovery of thy goods will be unexpected.

When thou hast proved thy friend, thou mayest truly trust and value him.

How expectest thou to live in the remembrance of thy fellow-mortals, seeing thy deeds are evil!

Let not caprice mar thy happiness.

Be not buoyed up by hopes of inheriting property which thou hast not earned.

Be prudent and success will attend thee.

Be contented with thy present fortune.

Fortune favours the brave and enterprising.

Thy adversary will cheat thee on the first opportunity.

Justice is blind, but not always deaf; for in many cases she loveth to listen to the sweet ringing of gold and silver.

Avoid entering into the land of strangers.

As thy youth may have been virtuous, so will thine old age prove respected and happy.

The captive will speedily cease to breathe the foul air of a dungeon; let him use his freedom wisely.

B

The door of the dungeon will be very speedily unlocked.

Consult thy present condition, whether it be right in thee to marry!

She shall have a son who shall gain much wealth and honour.

Thy friends are well and are now occupied in promoting thy welfare.

Thou must, and thou oughtest, to be on thy guard.

Choose that of thy richest relative.

Disappointment and vexation will attend thee, if thou neglectest thy calling, to look after that which is not within thy power to find.

Implore the aid of Providence, ere thou settest thy foot without the threshold of thy house.

The heart of thy beloved yearneth toward thee.

Let proper medicines be prescribed for the patient, and certain recovery will be the consequence.

Thy husband will have many virtues, but also some faults; teach him to correct the latter, and fortune will attend you both.

Thy character will be proof against every ill report

Let thy heart be cheered under thy misfortunes, for prosperity will return to thee in due season.

The signification is increase of riches.

Recovery from thy misfortunes will be gradual, but neglect no opportunity of honestly advancing thine own interests.

If thou wishest thy children to be happy, let thy precepts and practice be both in favour of virtue.

B

If misfortunes occur, bear them with fortitude, and happiness will be the certain issue.

Be thou constant, and fear not.

Matters which concern the absentee's future happiness, prevent his immediate return.

A conqueror of noble mind and mighty power, shall spring from low condition; he will break the chains of the oppressed, and will give liberty to the nations.

The thief will be detected in the midst of his career.

If thy friend hath in one circumstance proved deceitful, trust him not a second time.

The deeds of the evil-doer will be held in execration by posterity.

Take heed that avarice prove not the bane of thy happiness.

The will of a stranger may be written in thy favour.

Be not discouraged by adverse circumstances.

Be just in thy dealings, and trust to Providence for advancement.

Nothing venture, nothing win!

Bet nothing on the result of a game played by others.

God will support thee in a good cause.

Thy wealth will not be gained in a strange land.

The end of dissipation is speedy death – avoid this, and live long.

C

Early to bed, early to rise makes a man healthy, and wealthy, and wise.

The prisoner will speedily be released.

Good temper and fidelity are all thou mayest depend on.

She shall have a daughter who will inherit all her mother's virtues.

Sickness is not entirely absent from the mansion of those whom thou inquirest after; they say that thy presence would be agreeable.

Thou hast an enemy who will attempt to injure thee.

Tread in thy parents' footsteps.

Spend not thy substance in looking after that which is not.

Ere thou stirrest abroad, put thine affairs in order, and when thou returnest from thy journey, thou shalt find thy goods secure.

The love which ye bear each other will be rewarded by a happy marriage.

As thou hopest for a speedy recovery, follow not the advice of the tampering charlatan.

The man of thy heart will not be rich; but his person will be well favoured, and he will give thee every satisfaction.

No man ever was, or ever will be, without enemies; but those who slander thee shall be taken in their own nets.

If thou goest to a far country, thy lot will be to undergo many perils.

It portendeth death among thine enemies.

There be many who sink under the burdens of life – be not thou one of them: exert thyself and prosper.

C

As thou desirest prosperity and happiness for thy children, teach them to avoid evil company.

By this marriage, if thou art prudent, thou wilt gain much happiness.

Give no credit to the insinuation that thy beloved will prove untrue.

The absent traveller will very soon return in good health.

The Islanders who have long swayed the sceptre of the ocean, shall cease to conquer, but they will become the instructors of mankind.

Let not thy hopes of recovering what thou hast lost, be too sanguine.

If thou seest the man whom thou callest thy friend, act deceitfully toward others, deceive not thyself by thinking he will be faithful to thee.

Let not the love of fame blind thee to the interests of thy fellow creatures.

Thou shalt be happier than heretofore.

Be contented with what thou already hast in possession.

Fortune will shower her favours on thee, if thou couplest justice with prudence.

Hope still! Never despair!

Lose not thy time and money, by expecting from lotteries what thou mayest obtain from thy business.

When thy ready money is gone, go too; never borrow.

Thou shalt have no gain in a lawsuit; be therefore wise and careful.

In a strange land a very happy marriage awaits thee.

D

Thou shalt have to travel both by sea and by land.

Yes.

He will at last be freed from the power of his enemies.

Thou shalt have a fortune with thy partner.

Thou shalt be blessed with a son; who, if duly instructed, will make thine age honourable.

Thy friend enjoys perfect health, and is at present engaged in writing an epistle to a relative.

A secret enemy will endeavour to undermine your happiness.

Choose one, which, with little labour, will afford thee a comfortable subsistence.

Thy business will produce to thee a mine of wealth, if thou art but careful and improvest thy time.

Thy journey will be safe, and its object will be attained.

Thy love is not disregarded.

The patient will recover; but let this illness be a warning, in future, to keep due guard over his health.

Thou shalt wed a man on whom great honours will be conferred.

See that thou *deservest* to be well spoken of.

Great vicissitudes await the traveller.

The signification is disaster among thy foes.

D

Consider whether thou art not thyself the cause of thy misfortunes; if so, be more prudent for the future.

Misery will be the sure portion of thy children, if their morals be corrupted by evil communication.

Delay not this union, as thereby thy happiness would be retarded.

Thou shalt reign paramount in the affections of the being whom thou lovest.

Let not impatience urge too speedy a return.

As instruction is diffused throughout the world, men, of all conditions, all colours, will become free.

With trouble and expense thou mayest gain thy lost goods.

Honesty is the only bond of true friendship.

Seek not fame at the cannon's mouth.

Supreme felicity is very seldom the fate of mortal man.

Thou art the favourite of fortune.

Weigh well the probable result of thy present intentions.

By upright conduct thou art sure to rise.

Save pence; pounds will save themselves.

Never lend at the gaming table.

Rather sacrifice a shilling, than throw away a pound in litigation.

E

Do wisely, act justly, and trouble not the judges of the land.

It would be imprudent in thee to embark for a foreign land.

Some men are old even at thirty: take care of thy health, and thou wilt see threescore and ten.

The captive's heart will be made glad.

If thou art careful thou wilt marry exceedingly well.

Thy wife shall have two daughters, whose virtue and beauty will be the theme of general praise.

Thy friends are now carousing, and wishing thee health and happiness.

Beware of false friends!

Thou mayest write up, shave for a penny, cut hair for two-pence.

Vain man! flatter not thyself with the hopes of finding silver and gold in hidden places.

Let the companions of thy journey be honest as well as brave.

Heed not, if disappointment should mar thy present hopes.

The patient's health will be restored.

Thou shalt wed a man in an exalted station.

Do justly, and defy calumny.

If thou setteth forth from the land of thy fathers, expect great changes.

E

Thy dream sayeth be diligent in thy business.

Mankind are often the arbiters of their own fortunes; be honest, and fail not to take advantage of every circumstance that may improve thine.

Destroy the seeds of vice, and implant those of virtue in the minds of thy children, and happiness will be the certain issue.

Bethink thee whether thou oughtest now to marry.

Constancy on thy part will meet a due return.

When the object is accomplished, the traveller will assuredly return.

A colony of outcasts will break their chains, and obtain great dominion.

Let not the loss of this thing press heavily on thy mind.

Rely not on those self-styled friends, who, like summer flies, buzz about thee in thy prosperity.

A cottage and content give more enjoyment than the princely palace of the overturner of kingdoms.

Be contented with thy lot, and there is little doubt of thy happiness.

Be content: let to-morrow provide for itself.

As thou hopest for success, act not unjustly toward others.

Cast not away thy present prospects in pursuing a phantom.

In thy family be liberal, but in thy business save even a farthing; four farthings make a penny.

Preserve the greatest equanimity at the gaming table!

F

Money may be staked, but goods and lands ought never to be risked at the gaming table.

Thou shalt be involved in a suit; but speedily extricate thyself.

Thou wilt be truly prosperous in thy journey; but stay not abroad longer than is necessary.

Rise early, work or walk before you eat, and doubt it not.

The prisoner will soon have cause to rejoice.

Thy partner will be rich; but she will also be proud.

She shall bear a son, whose talents will be of the first order; see that they be well directed.

The health of those thou lovest is good; they enjoy the sweets of rural happiness, and wish that thou wert with them.

Thou hast enemies, but they will possess no power over thee.

Meddle not with the laws of the land.

If thou payest attention to all the departments of thy calling, a fortune awaits thee, greater than any treasure in the country in which thou residest.

Tempt not these whom thou meetest, or hast to deal with, by showing unto them thy money-bags

If thy love is true it will be duly appreciated.

A speedy recovery will be the consequence of properly applied remedies.

Thy husband will be in all respects a good man; it will be his study to render thee the happiest of thy sex.

Let thy conduct be unimpeachable, and thou mayest defy the slanderous tongue.

F

Be prudent, and do not depend entirely on thy present good fortune.

Thou wert desired in thy vision to give some of thy superfluity in charity to the poor.

Thy present misfortunes shall have but little influence on thy future fortune.

When thou art cold in thy grave, thy name will be greatly honoured in thy children.

By wedding this person thou ensurest happiness for a long season.

If thy beloved hath proved inconstant to another, think not that she will prove faithful to thee.

Love prompts the traveller's speedy return to his home.

An infant nation shall, by the wisdom of its councils, become the emporium of commerce and the arts.

Thy goods may soon be recovered.

Give out that thou art poor, and see how many, or what friends, will run to serve thee.

Be not the trumpeter of thine own fame; if thy deeds are truly great, posterity will not overlook them.

Whatever occurs, be not discontented.

Hope for the best, but make up thy mind to bear with the worst that may happen.

Save thyself the trouble and expense of entering into a rash and unprofitable speculation.

Be content, and heed not the goadings of wicked ambition.

Parsimony is hateful; yet, a groat saved each day amounts to more than six pounds a year.

G

Be like the bee, and thou shalt gather the honey of industry.

Thou wilt mar it wondrously.

To avoid this great evil, depends principally on thyself.

Thy journey, when thou goest, will be much to thy advantage.

Long life depends greatly on temperance.

He who inhabits the dungeon, will escape.

Thy first partner will be young, handsome and chaste; thy second, exactly the reverse.

A daughter will be born unto thee, who will possess much beauty; which may prove a snare to her, if early vanity be not duly checked.

Thy friends are not in ill-health, but all things are not at present agreeable to them.

Envious persons will endeavour to impede thy passage through life.

Avoid edge-tools!

Be diligent in thy calling, and puff not thy mind up with false hopes.

As thou journeyest along, commend thyself to God, and he will watch over thee.

If thou art discreet, thou shalt gain the suit in which thy heart is fixed.

Let the advice of the experienced be taken, and health will speedily be restored.

Thou shalt marry a man whose mind will be elevated above his condition. It will be thy duty sometimes to restrain him.

G

It will! but out of their own mouths will thy slanderers be condemned.

Despair not; though fortune should desert thee, it will but be for a time.

Thou wert told in thy vision, that thy present undertaking will prosper; if thou art cautious and vigilant.

Cheer thy heart, prosperity will soon attend thee.

Chose those callings for thy children, for which their talents are adapted; teach them to be virtuous and prudent, and leave the result to God.

Enter not into a state, of which thou hast not well considered the end.

Thy beloved meriteth all thy confidence.

Nothing can happen to retard the stranger's speedy arrival.

The rank weeds which have long infested the gardens of the south, will be plucked out, and the tree of liberty will flourish luxuriantly in their stead.

Leave no means untried to detect the thief.

The man who boasts his readiness to befriend thee will, in adversity, be the first to desert thee.

Dip not thy green laurels in the blood of the vanquished.

Let not the irritation of thy temper mar thy happiness.

Be courteous to thy kinsman, and he will remember thee.

Take the advice of thy best friend before thou proceedest.

Thou shalt long be prosperous, and thou oughtest therewith to be content; in the end, thy unbounded ambition will be thy ruin.

H

Thou shalt be fortunate, and meet with preferment in thy business.

Yes!

Dost thou expect to plunge thy hand into the fire and not be burnt?

Do as thou wouldest be done by, and thou wilt save much time and money.

Venture not far from home.

Go to bed with the lamb, rise with the lark, and doubt it not.

A friend will procure his speedy release.

Thy partner's temper will be exemplary; take care that in all cases, thou imitatest it.

Thy wife shall have a son, who will be both learned and virtuous.

Amusement at present occupies the attention of thy friends.

Thou hast an enemy but thy person and fortune are safe from every attempt at doing thee harm.

If thou art truly wise, thou wilt not spurn rural felicity.

A treasure awaits thee of which thou hast little expectation.

Danger may threaten thee if thou sojournest long in a strange land.

The hand of thy beloved will ultimately reward thy affection.

Though the patient escape this time, let him not presume on the strength of his constitution.

H

By thy marriage thou wilt be envied by others of thy sex.

Be prudent and courteous to all men, and the arrows of slander will be blunted before they reach thee.

It will be thy fate to see many changes.

Thou dreamedst of a wedding which will soon take place.

See that thy misfortunes urge thee not into drunkenness :– if so, thou wilt never recover from them.

In the training of thy offspring, let thy discipline be strict, but not severe; lose no opportunity of improving their understandings, and in the plenitude of their happiness they will bless thee.

It behooves the party to make a light matter of any impediments which may be thrown in the way of his happiness.

There is no just cause why thou shouldest question the fidelity of the beloved of thy heart.

Though the stranger's stay abroad be long, it will be greatly to his advantage.

When imbecility and folly are laid low, a powerful people will regard the liberty they have lost.

Take not away the life of a man who has injured thee.

Avoid laying too great a tax on the patience of thy friends :– this is the way to preserve them.

Be not eager to rear the monument of thy own fame.

Matrimony will afford thee much happiness.

Be civil to every man; thou knowest not who may prove thy friend.

Be not purse – proud nor vain – glorious in the midst of thy good fortunes.

I

Let the star of prudence guide thee in thy course.

There is a tide in the affairs of men, which taken at the flood, leads on to fortune.

Thou shalt not :– but be content and happy.

Taste not! touch not! handle not!

If thou dislikest the law, meddle not with it.

When thou hast occasion, thou mayest proceed confidentially.

Old age is attained only by the man who has the resolution to live temperately.

The prisoner will soon be welcomed home, although he now smarts under the power of his enemies.

Thou shalt have a handsome partner.

She shall have a son, whose dutiful conduct in his youth will ensure thee comfort in thine age.

Thy friends are now occupied in devotional duties.

Enemies will endeavour to subvert thy good reputation.

Sell strong liquors; but be careful of often trying their strength upon thyself.

A rich treasure awaits thee.

No accident will befall thee.

Thou art more beloved than thou canst be now aware of.

I

The afflicted will soon be free from pain.

Thy husband will inherit great riches.

Thou wilt be calumniated, but when thy slanderers are confronted they will be put to shame.

Political changes, will change thy fortune.

Thy vision portendeth, that gifts will be made unto thee.

Strong drink may cheer thy heart now, and make thee forget thy sorrows for a short season; but in the end they will unfit thee for the enjoyment of prosperity.

Lose no opportunity of pointing out to thy children the deeds of virtuous men, and in their emulation of them they will do honour to thy precepts.

Much prosperity will attend the wedded pair.

Harbour not unjust suspicions.

When the stranger hath settled his affairs, he will lose no time in returning to his own country.

The deluder of his people will be caught in the meshes of the cunningly contrived net which he himself hath woven.

Give not the thief the chance of again robbing thee.

Consider well, ere thou tellest thy secret, whether thy friend can keep it.

Do good, and if mankind should fail to remember thee, thou art still their benefactor.

Think not of enjoying happiness while thy conduct needs reformation.

Be a friend to thyself: depend not on others.

J

Wish not for the death of thy kinsman, that thou mayest inherit his worldly goods.

Avarice is the ruin of thousands.

Perseverance conquers every impediment.

Thou art too ambitious.

Thou mayest yet be successful: millions have been ruined.

Thy fate is to litigate, but in the end thou wilt be successful.

If thou tarriest long from thy home, thy fortune will not prosper.

Drunkenness brings on premature old age; avoid it, and you will live long.

With much difficulty he will obtain a discharge from his prison.

Your partner will, in time, have much money:– use it well.

A daughter will be born unto thee, who will be highly honoured and respected.

Thy friend is well; he now drinketh thy health.

Thou hast enemies; but thou shalt defeat them, and they will be overwhelmed with shame.

Thou mayest make a fortune by dealing in precious stones.

Health will be to thee richest treasure thou canst ever possess.

Safety and success in thy travels, will greatly depend upon thy conduct toward those whom thou meetest.

J

Persevere and give not thy suit up lightly.

Let all proper means be used, and a speedy end will be put to the patient's disorder.

By marriage, thy fortune and happiness will be greatly increased.

When the evil report reacheth thine ears, instantly find the slanderer out, and he will be confounded in thy presence.

Whatever changes thou mayst undergo, they will be for thy benefit.

It sayeth that favours will be conferred on thee forthwith.

As thou hopest for lasting prosperity, drown not thy cares in strong drink; if thou dost, thy prospects will be forever blasted.

Their happiness will depend solely on the instruction which thou givest them.

Be discreet in the connection which thou formest for life.

The suspicious lover is the destroyer of his own peace.

When the absentee returns, it will be with Joy and honour.

Ignorance and oppression, like a thick mist on he mountain top, will be gradually dispersed, as he sun of knowledge enlightens the understanding of men.

Admonish, but pursue not unto death, him who hath injured thee.

Never trust those men who swear friendship to thee over the cup of drunkenness.

The good deeds of men are frequently traced on sand; their bad ones graven on marble.

Set not thy heart on pleasures derived from terrestrial objects.

K

Peace and plenty will be thy certain portion, if thou art industrious.

Whilst thou waitest for dead men's old shoes, thine own exertions might procure thee new ones.

Let prudence guide thee in this affair.

Preferment depends entirely on thyself.

Doubt it not.

The chances are three to one against thee.

Avoid law as thou wouldest the pestilence.

In another country fortune will shower her favours on thee.

Length of days depends greatly on thy habits ;– if thou dost not gormandize, nor tipple, thou wilt live long in the land.

The prisoner will find much difficulty in obtaining pardon.

Thou wilt marry into a rich and respectable family.

A beautiful male child will be born unto thee.

Thy friend is happier and in better health than usual; and is preparing for a journey.

Thou wilt be invested by secret enemies, but they will be caught in the trap which they prepared for thee.

Be a miller, but grind not the faces of the poor.

Thou shalt possess a rich mine, out of which treasures shall be dug from time to time.

K

Prosperity will surely attend thee.

Consider whether the object of thy affections doth deserve thy love.

Fear not but that the patient will recover.

Thy husband will be a man of honour and integrity.

Thy reputation will not be seriously injured by calumny.

Look not on the present as the most important period of thy life.

It signifieth prosperity to thee and thine.

When thy misfortunes press hardest on thee, be not dismayed, but endeavour to remove them.

If thy child be permitted to stray from the paths of virtue, thou mayest expect that vice and misery will be his portion through life.

Marriages patched up hastily end in sorrow : not so those which are prudently contracted.

The object of thy affections will never return thy love with ingratitude.

Fear not but that the stranger will very speedily return.

Shouts of "Freedom !" will resound throughout the halls which once were filled with the sighs and groans of despair.

Leave no means untried to make good thy loss.

Beware lest the honied words of the hypocrite and the deceiver betray thee into danger.

Take good heed ! - infamy is the certain portion of the wicked man.

L

Thy name will be handed down with the memory of thy deeds to the most distant posterity.

There is every prospect of happiness for thee.

Depend not entirely on the present intentions of thy kinsman :– they may alter.

Success will depend much on perseverance.

Thou shalt meet with many obstacles, but at length thou shalt attain the highest earthly power and honour.

Industry, perseverance, and circumspection accomplish thy most sanguine wishes.

Play no games of hazard.

Law is a two-edged sword, which will assuredly smite thee, if thou comest within its reach.

Remain at home, and thou wilt do well.

A frugal repast will preserve thy health, and give thee many days to live; whilst the midnight banquet may kill thee straight.

Once more will the captive breathe the air of freedom.

Thy partner will be strictly virtuous ;– see to it that thou be so likewise.

Thou shalt have a son, whose health in his childhood will require much care.

Thy friends are making merry, and wish thee to form one of their circle.

Thou hast; but they will be discomfitted.

Thou art cut out for a rope-dancer.

L

Contentment is a richer treasure than any other you can find.

Associate not thyself with wicked companions, and thy journey will be accomplished in safety.

Wait patiently, and thy love will be requited in due season.

Let not old women, who pretend to medical knowledge, tamper with the patient's constitution.

Thy husband's conduct will be such as to merit from thee every kindness.

If thou actest prudently and uprightly, thou needest not fear the tongue of the slanderer.

As the seasons vary, so will thy fortune.

It sayeth, let not the next opportunity escape of advancing thy fortune.

Let not despair be added to the burden of thy misfortunes, but hope that they will be removed in due time.

If thou gainest the confidence of thy children, thou mayest lay the foundation of their happiness, by teaching them to discriminate between good and evil.

If avarice, or mere lust, tempt thy marriage, expect not lasting happiness.

As the sun steadily pursueth his glorious course in the heavens, so will thy beloved remain constant in her vows.

Thou shalt soon behold the face of the stranger.

A vast empire in the west will burst the chains which fetter it.

If thou art careful the property may soon be found.

The grip of the hand, the kiss on the cheek, and the vow of friendship over the flowing bowl, are but as words traced on the sand of the sea-shore :– trust them not.

M

Place not thy confidence so much even in a friend, as to put a weapon in his hand which he may, in future, turn upon thyself.

Thy fame will resound to the farthest corner of the earth.

Prosperity awaits thee.

Thine own industry will supply every want: but if property be bequeathed thee, be thankful.

If thou managest discreetly, thou shalt be successful.

Thou shalt be preferred.

In ten years from this time (unless by too little dependence on thyself, thou drive fortune from thy door) thou shalt be called a rich man.

If thou art wise, give to the poor, what thou art content to throw away on the turn of a card.

Law leaves little for the litigant ;– thou wilt gain thy cause, but the cost will be greater than it is worth.

Tarry with thy friends and thou wilt escape many calamities.

The shipwrecked mariner may escape the raging billows, and the thief the gallows-tree; but sudden death is the sure portion of the glutton and the drunkard.

If much exertion be used, he will obtain his liberty.

A rich and young person will be thy partner.

She shall have a son, who will reflect much honour on his family.

Thy friend is free from all bodily illness, and now listeneth to the sweet sounds of music.

The enemies who conspire against thee will be brought to shame and punishment.

M

Thou mayest be a merchant: but sell not thy soul for gain.

It will be thy fate to pass by, but not to find, a treasure.

Put not thy trust in the fair appearance of all those whom thou meetest in thy travels.

Thou art sincerely beloved.

Let not expense be an obstacle to the restoration of the patient's health.

Consider well whether thou oughtest, at present, to change thy condition in life.

Be more careful to deserve a good reputation by acting virtuously, than merely to avoid the petty calumnies of the envious slanderer.

It is decreed that thy life will be checkered by many viscissitudes; but ultimately, thou shalt enjoy peace and comfort.

It signifieth a gift from a far country.

Thy misfortunes are but temporary.

Point out to thy children the deformity of vice, and they will shun it.

When thou art wed, insist not so much on prerogative, but let each yield a little.

Let not distrust mar thy happiness.

When the time of his sojourning in a foreign land is past, he will return.

As the volcano bursts with a louder explosion when the combustible matter is confined within its bosom, so will a nation's revenge find vent, the more their wrongs are repressed.

The person who hath wronged thee will be cut off in the midst of his wickedness.

N

The thief may be successful for a time, but in the end is certain death.

Be exceedingly cautious in the choice of thy friend.

Let thy deeds deserve praise, and posterity will applaud them.

The harvest of plenty and happiness is ready; thou must reap it with the sickle of industry.

Bless the memory of the giver!

Be on thy guard against unforseen events.

Be contented with thy present lot.

Enter into no rash speculations.

Be warned! from henceforth, never play for money nor money's worth.

When thou understandest thoroughly the grounds of thy suit, proceed justly and in the end thou wilt triumph.

If thou art prudent, fortune awaits thee openhanded, in another country.

O man! if thou wouldest see length of days, eschew drunkenness, gluttony, and all intemperance.

The prisoner's release is uncertain :– let some kinsman interest him in his behalf.

Thou wilt marry one who hath before tasted the sweets of matrimony.

She will have a son who will live to a great age.

Thy friends are in good health; they have just heard news from a far country.

N

Enemies thou hast; but their designs will be frustrated.

Love not gold so much as to be an usurer.

If thou takest care to acquire knowledge, it will prove a rich treasure, of which no one can deprive thee.

When thou hast arrived at thy place of destination, lose no time in executing thy errand, and return without delay.

Thou shalt receive proofs that thou art beloved.

Put faith in no advice save that of experience.

Thy husband's talents will promote him to honour and to great trust.

At one period of thy existence, attempts will be made to misrepresent thy conduct in the eyes of the world.

A peaceful life is ordained for thee.

It importeth health and happiness.

Be not discouraged; though thou art now engulfed in misfortune, thy spirits will soon be buoyed up by prosperity.

Discourage deceit in thy child; but at the same time teach him prudence that he may not be deceived by others.

To bear and forbear, is the grand secret of matrimonial happiness.

Take heed that jealousy prove not the bane of thy happiness.

The traveller will return richly laden.

Whilst the winds are still, and the air serene, the earth may quake suddenly, and those on its surface be swallowed up.

O

After much rain, there will be a plentiful harvest.

Exert thyself manfully to recover the property which thou hast lost.

Try thy friend before thou trustest him too deeply.

If thy deeds are evil, posterity will execrate thy name.

Let not thy exertions flag, and thou wilt be prosperous.

See that thou art not cheated out of thy just rights.

Fear not, if thou art prudent.

Thou shalt be exalted above thy fellows.

Mind what thou art about, and thou art sure to be successful.

If it will afford thee pleasure to behold thyself and family reduced from comfort to beggary–play!

Send thy cause before a jury of thy countrymen.

If thou remainest in thine own country, thou mayest still be successful.

I have seen the rich man bestow all his goods in charity, and have known the sun to be wholly darkened, but have never yet beheld the hoary locks and healthy aspect of an intemperate man.

Enlargement for the unfortunate captive!

A rich partner, but of a very bad temper.

A son will be born unto thee who will possess great riches.

O

Thy friends are well, but have anxiety concerning thee.

Be thou vigilant, and the designs of those who would do thee mischief will be defeated.

Knowest thou that, which in the shortest time will be productive of most profit to thee?

It is decreed that thou shalt find another's property; but it behooves thee to restore it to the right owner.

Those who are with thee, will guard over thy safety.

Give further proofs of attachment to thy beloved, and a due return will be made thee.

The patient may look forward to length of days.

Many of thy sex will envy thee the possession of so comely and so kind a husband.

The slanderous reports of thine enemies will not affect the stability of thy reputation.

When thou least expectest, a beneficial change will take place in thy fortune.

It signifieth recovery from illness.

Apply thyself steadily to improve thy fortune, and success will crown thy endeavour.

Train thy child in the way in which he should walk, and when he is old he will not depart from it.

It is folly in thee to wed, if thou hast nothing but mere beauty, or love to feed upon.

Live cheerily, work merrily, watch warily, but suspect not lightly.

Riches, happiness, and honour, will be in the train of the returning stranger.

P

Thy hopes for the stranger's speedy return are not well grounded.

The governments of nations be very speedily changed.

Punish not the delinquent too severely.

Thy friend will assuredly prove faithful to thee. Is he thy friend?

Be honest, and content with the praise of thy contemporaries.

Fail not by persevering industry, to fill thy barns with grain, thy purse with money, in case of need.

When thou takest possession of the worldly goods of the deceased, do justice to the widow and the orphan.

Venture not rashly.

Thy preferment will be owing to thine own deserts.

When thou hast amassed £10,000–retire.

Why stake thy fortune, thy happiness, thy very existence, on the cast of a die, or the turn of a card?

Be thou thine own advocate.

When thou dost travel, providence will protect thee.

Thou wilt fondle over the children's children.

After long imprisonment he will be released.

Your partner will be a pattern of virtue and beauty.

P

Thou shalt have a son, who shall inherit all his mother's accomplishments and his father's virtues.

Doubt not but that thy friends are well and happy; they now relish the sweets of a simple but plentiful repast.

The designs of the man who will become thine enemy shall not prevail against thee.

Follow the plough.

Thou shalt assuredly find something, but it will not be of much value to thee.

Linger not unnecessarily on the road, lest danger befall thee.

Thou art beloved: but improve the opportunity, for delays are dangerous.

A speedy abatement will take place in the patient's disorder.

The mind and the complexion of thy husband will be that of the fox; his practices those of the wolf.

The slander which is uttered against thee, will not be credited.

Be not dismayed if misfortune should overtake thee; she will not long keep thee company.

It saith thou hast enemies who are endeavouring to render thee unhappy.

Thy misfortunes are not so great, but that thy own exertions may relieve thee.

Cherish the seeds of virtue in thy children, and doubt not but in age, they will reap the harvest of happiness.

Exert thyself to make thy partner happy, and thou shalt thyself be so likewise.

Absence will effect no change in the sentiments of the beloved of thy soul.

Q

The heart which is penetrated by love for thee, will prove true.

He will soon return, to the great joy of all his friends.

A southern nation will speedily undergo a change in its government for the better.

A clean corner is not the worse for being twice searched.

Be thine own friend.

Let not a love of fame prompt thee to wicked deeds.

Thy future happiness depends upon thyself.

What hast thou to do with legacies? Be industrious and frugal.

Consider well before thou venturest further in this scheme.

Thine own merits will exalt thee.

Do riches bring content and happiness?

Do not bet high.

Submit to no arbitration, but abide by the verdict of an honest jury.

Thy journey will be prosperous if guided by prudence.

Thou shalt be termed venerable – see that thy long life be spent usefully.

The bolts will be drawn, the door opened, and the chain will be broken.

Q

Thy partner will not be handsome, but there be no other cause for dislike.

A son will be born unto thee, who shall possess much power.

The health of thy friend requireth not the physician's aid; he peruseth a letter just received, which giveth much satisfaction.

An enemy will endeavour to mar thy prospects; he will be taken in the net which he hath spread for thee.

Seek not the honour nor the dangers of the field.

A good-humoured mate will be a treasure, which thy eyes will delight to look upon.

The companion of thy travels will be unto thee a shield against every danger.

Thou hast the love of others beside that of the darling of thy heart.

Let not the patient be afflicted by melancholy anticipations.

Thy husband will sit in high places.

Evil reports will be uttered against thee, but in due season the slanderer will be discovered, and brought to punishment.

Look well to it, that the lessons which thou receiveth in Misfortune's school may be useful to thee when thou art prosperous.

It signifieth that thou wilt soon hear agreeable news.

Be patient now, and in after seasons, prudent. Thus only canst thou attain prosperity and happiness.

Chastise thy child when he doth evil, and in the end he will have cause to bless thy name.

Examine strictly the disposition of thy intended partner, and if it accord with thine own, fear not but happiness will attend you both.

R

Those who observe truly the vows that have been sworn at the altar need not fear unhappiness.

Question not the constancy of thy beloved.

He will not return at the time expected.

The present age teems with events of much political importance.

Seek, and thou shalt find.

Trust not even a friend with a secret which ought remain within thy own breast.

Though the present generation may flatter thee, the succeeding one may not be so courteous.

Place not thy happiness in store of gold and silver; but in all thy dealings preserve thy conscience pure and undefiled.

Hope for the best!

Be not buoyed up by the success which may be thy portion.

As the Nile produceth abundant harvests by its annual overflow, so will the good-will of a friend produce thee preferment, fortune and honour.

Thy speculations will be generally successful.

A lucky hit may make thy fortune :– if so, play more.

Endeavour to accommodate all differences by the private arbitration of mutual friends.

Thou shalt tarry where thou now residest.

Thou shalt live long; let not thy years be passed ingloriously.

R

The fettered will soon be free.

A rich partner is ordained for you.

Thou shalt have a daughter, who will possess a noble mind and amiable manners.

The friend whom thou inquirest after, is in good health, and is now locked in the arms of sleep.

See that thy present friends do not become thy determined foes.

Take physic when there is need; but presume not to give it to others.

Be industrious ; and place no reliance on such phantasies.

Boast not on the road of the riches which thou carriest with thee, lest they be coveted by others.

Thou art adored but lose not thy 'vantage ground by inattention or procrastination.

Let strict attention be paid to the directions given by the medical attendant.

Thy husband shall have rule and direction over affairs of great importance.

Give not the slanderer an opportunity of injuring thy reputation.

When thou hast enough, therewith be content, and seek not to enlarge thy store by venturing further.

It signifieth plenty of everything which gold can purchase.

Though thou art poor and needy, purchase not prosperity by any sacrifice of honesty or honour;– fortune's wheel is constantly turning.

Neglect no opportunity of cultivating the minds of thy children, and their journey through life will be virtuous and happy.

S

Commit the several members of thy family to care of an all-seeing Providence, and he will protect them.

Mutual love will secure prosperity and real happiness.

Be as constant to thy beloved as she is to thee, and thou mayest be happy.

The stranger will return unexpectedly.

The prudent man will make provision against every change that may take place.

Make proper inquiries, and they may lead to detection.

Show thy friend, by good treatment of him, that it is his interest to be faithful to thee.

Desire not to attain immortality by the vices of reckless ambition.

Brood not over thy misfortunes, but exert thyself the future.

Good fortune is in store for thee.

Keep thine own counsel, and success will attend thee.

Neglect not the opportunities which may be offered to thee, for they will lead to great preferment.

A partner in thy business would ruin thee.

Never throw good money after bad.

With the blessing of God thou shalt gain thy cause.

Wander not far from thy home.

S

Providence watches over thee, and will lengthen thy days, if thou avoidest the sin of drunkenness.

After a short time all anxiety for the prisoner will cease.

Thou wilt be exceedingly fortunate in thy marriage.

A son will be born, who, if he receive not timely correction, may prove a source of trouble to thee.

The object of thy solicitude is as well in health as thou couldest wish, and is now engaged in domestic occupations.

Beware of treachery! Nothing further may be now revealed to thee.

Cultivate thy talents, and adopt a profession supported by fees.

Thou mayest; but be not disappointed if it be of not great value.

Set out one day, sooner or later, than thou hadst previously intended.

Your love is mutual, but endeavours will be made to cause dissension between you.

To ensure recovery, the patient's mind must be kept in cheerful mood, by the conversation of those who are most beloved.

Thou shalt wed a man of high birth, but little fortune.

Let justice and prudence be the guardians of reputation.

The early part of thy career will be subject to viscissitudes, but in thy age thou shalt enjoy uninterrupted happiness.

It warneth thee to beware of danger.

Sit not down under thy misfortunes, wringing thy hands, and accusing the justice of Providence; but up, and be doing, and fortune will again smile upon thee.

T

As the tall column is exalted above the petty ruins which surround its base, so shalt thou rise superior to thy present misfortunes.

If thou hast been prudent and just, thy family will follow thy example and be happy.

Confidence in each other will ensure happiness.

The heart of thy beloved will find room for no other object but thyself.

The stranger will return at the time thou expectest him.

If the season be unfavourable, let thy exertions be the greater.

Despair not of recovering thy goods.

Wrangle not with thy friend about trifles, else thou mayest forfeit his assistance in matters of great import.

Do justice rather for justice's sake, than to be praised in future ages.

Anticipate not misfortunes before their time.

The money which will be left thee will not remunerate thy anxiety.

Seek the assistance of a wiser man than thyself.

Eminence is attained by the proper culture of great talents, and preferment by interest; thy lot is cast between both.

Take a partner, but be not thyself a sleeping one.

Visit a gaming house, behold the despair of the gamester who has just lost his all – and then play.

Thou shalt be foiled by the opponent's cunning devices.

T

In a foreign land strangers will protect and cherish thee.

Desire not so much length of days, as to improve the time which God giveth thee on earth.

The prisoner ought to sue for pardon and mercy.

By this marriage you will soon obtain great property.

Thy progeny shall be both male and female; they will be the staff and comfort of thy age.

Thy friend whom thou inquirest after is in excellent health, and is now engaged in a conversation with a relative.

An enemy will try to circumvent thee, but he will be foiled in his attempts.

Follow the bent of thine own inclination.

Domestic felicity will be of more value to thee than the contents of ten thousand mines of gold, silver, and precious stones.

Be not dismayed if thou shouldest meet with danger; it will not affect thee if thou art resolute.

The heart of thy beloved beateth responsive to the anxious throbbings of thine.

It is useless to look for relief from medicine, unless it be skilfully applied.

The man whom thou weddest shall have great power ;– teach him to use it rightly.

When thou art unjustly accused, thy innocence will thereby be confirmed, and the slanderers will be confounded.

Expect not to pass through life without a mixture of good and evil.

It portendeth a happy union between a man and woman, who have long loved each other.

U

Thy nightly visions portend good fortune to thee.

Thy misfortunes shall soon have an end.

Instruct thy children; show them a good example; and fear not for their happiness.

The marriage will prove both prosperous and happy.

Another will attempt to supplant thee in the affections of the being whom thou tenderly lovest.

The stranger cannot return at present.

The earth will be fertilized by abundance of rain.

Art thou certain that it hath been stolen?

Reckon not much on the friendship of any man.

Fulfil the duties of thy station, and care not for the unprofitableness of future fame.

If thou continuest virtuous thou shalt be happy.

Depend not on the caprice of age.

Look before thou leapest.

When thou enjoyest prosperity and honour, feel for the misfortunes of thy former friends.

Have a strict eye over those who eat thy bread.

The companion of blacklegs, cheats and thieves, even with a fortune, is never respected.

U

Venture freely in thy next cause, and gain will crown thy wishes.

Abide thy fate at home it will be better for thee.

Longevity is a curse to those who misspend life.

The prisoner will still pass many days in confinement.

Your matrimonial connections will not produce much happiness.

Sons and daughters will be the reward of the love which ye bear each other.

Thy friend is now in the act of paying a visit, and is both well and happy.

Thou hast little cause to dread the rage of any enemy who shall come against thee.

Be one of thy country's defenders.

One of thy kindred will find articles of great value.

The object of thy journey will be attained without hazard.

The heart of thy beloved wavereth between thee and another; improve the opportunities that will be offered thee.

The patient may still hope for health and long life.

Thy husband's fame will be exalted.

Thy innocence will uphold thee in the day of trial, and the tongue of the slanderer will forever be silenced.

Thy voyage through life will at first be boisterous; but the tempest will cease, and propitious winds will waft thee into the haven of independence.

V

Thou shalt be subject to a frequent change of residence.

Thy dream signifies that thou shouldest bestow some of thy goods in charity.

Be not dispirited by misfortunes; they will vanish as the thick mist is dissipated by the genial rays of the reviving sun.

As thou sowest, so shall thy children reap.

Let no petty bickerings disturb the felicity of the married state.

Thy beloved will not cease to pray for thy speedy return.

He will return in due season.

Expect a plentiful harvest.

The thief shall ultimately be detected.

Sad is his fate who relies solely on the friendship and good-will of others.

Whilst thou seekest to obtain fame, take heed that infamy may not be thy portion.

As the sun revives the flowers of the field, so wilt prosperity in thy business make thy heart glad.

Blessed is he who expecteth little, for he will not be disappointed.

Examine thyself strictly, whether thou oughtest not to abandon thy present intentions.

When thou enjoyest the favour of powerful men, let not thy pride be puffed up.

Thou wilt be the architect of thy own fortune; depend on no created being.

V

Be not intoxicated with good fortune at first :— that is the bait which is thrown out by the gamester to allure his prey.

If thou art cozened out of thy upper garment, cast not away thy under one to recover it.

Let not thy inordinate desire of amassing wealth carry thee into foreign climes.

Desire not to attain old age, if thy mind be not well stored with knowledge :— no wretch is so truly wretched as the ignorant old man.

Some one will pity and release the prisoner.

You will have every cause to love your partner.

A numerous offspring will be born unto thee :— if thou trainest them properly, their virtues will reward thy anxious toil.

Thy friend is free from all bodily affliction, and expecteth to receive a letter or news from thee.

In a contest which may soon take place, thou shalt be victorious over thine avowed enemies.

Thou wouldest cut but a sorry figure in the pulpit.

Snatch not at shadows; for thou mayest thereby lose the substance.

If thou meetest danger, face it boldly and be not daunted by appearances.

Fear not that another will supplant thee in the affections of the beloved of thy soul.

The patient's mind must not be afflicted by doleful intelligence.

Peace, plenty and happiness, will attend thy marriage with the beloved of thy heart.

Deal openly, prudently, and honestly, and then mayest thou defy the breath of the slanderer.

W

But few persons escape the envenomed tongue of slander.

Thou shalt meet with few difficulties.

The interpretation is, that thou shalt receive an epistle of importance.

Thine own exertions will enable thee to overcome every misfortune which may happen.

Lead thy children in the paths of righteousness, and when thou art gone, they will not depart from it.

Happiness depends solely on the affection and forbearance of both parties.

There is danger in long absence from the object of thy affection.

Matters of import prevent his immediate return.

A revolutionary spirit is abroad among the nations of the earth.

Be patient, and every circumstance will be developed.

If a man protesteth never-ceasing friendship for thee, at least doubt his sincerity.

Sully not thy laurels by unjust deeds.

Carry thyself prudently and justly, and thou wilt surely be happy.

Let not disappointment mar thy exertions in thy calling.

Fortune will attend thee,

When thou art in the zenith of thy power, let not unjust deeds procure thy downfall.

W

Give not large interest for money in thy business.

If thou playest, play fair, and see that others do the same.

There is great hinderance to thy present success in law matters.

Emigration from thy native land will but retard thy fortune.

Vain mortal! What wouldest thou? Hoary locks are the reward of temperance and virtue.

Try to unlock the dungeon by means of a golden key.

Be wary, and this marriage may prove very fortunate.

She shall have a son, who in his youth will be admired, and in his old age respected.

Thy friends labour under no bodily affliction, but they are not free from cares concerning worldly matters.

Thy enemies are powerless, and unworthy of thy regard.

On this subject take the advice last given thee by thy best friend.

In this, fortune hath not marked thee for her favourite.

In thy journey, fancy not that from each brake a robber or a tiger will spring upon thee, but pursue thy way steadily.

Success will attend thy anxious hopes, if thou art discreet in this matter.

A speedy cure will depend much on the patience with which the afflicted bears the present illness.

Thy husband will be a man well willed, with a house well filled, and a farm well tilled.

X

Thy husband will be learned, his temper good, and his complexion fair.

Thy slanderers will sooner or later be overwhelmed with shame and disgrace.

If thou tarriest at home, thou shalt meet with few changes.

Thy dream portendeth ill luck to thine enemies.

Thy misfortunes will cease to overpower thee.

Have more anxiety to bequeath knowledge than riches to thy children, and they will be happy.

This union will be productive of real happiness.

Be not neglectful, and thy beloved will remain true.

The traveller will speedily revisit his own country and kindred.

Despotism will be speedily overturned in a country long oppressed by illiterate, indolent, and luxurious strangers.

Make diligent inquiries amongst the members of thy house.

Rely more on the actions than on the promises of thy friends.

The good deeds of the virtuous only, will be held in esteem by posterity.

Thy misfortunes will vanish and thou shalt be happy.

Follow thy calling diligently, and be not a legacy hunter.

Rejoice at the fortune which is ordained for thee, and therewith be content.

X

When thou enjoyest the favour of the mighty men of the earth, take heed that thou art not ruined by a flattering tongue.

Deal honestly, and trust to God for success.

Mind thy business, and forsake the gaming table.

Give not large fees in this suit.

In a far country shalt thou find treasure.

If thou art temperate in thine appetite, cleanly in thy person, and just in thy dealings, the winter of thy age will run smoothly.

The captive will suffer no bodily affliction.

This marriage will add to your welfare and happiness.

She will have a son of a froward disposition; but it is thy business to correct and counsel him aright.

Thy friend is in good health, and hath some thought of going on a journey.

Thou hast enemies who will speak ill of thee, and who would otherwise injure thee.

Deal in books, and be prosperous.

A good name will prove to thee a treasure of great value :– see thou lose it not.

Tarry not unnecessarily on thy journey – delays may prove dangerous to thy safety.

A return of affection is at present doubtful, but perseverance and attention will ensure thee success.

Let the patient's mind be soothed by the kind and ready attention of friends, and the happiest result may be anticipated.

Y

The patient may recover; but in case of the worst due preparation ought to be made for the tomb.

Thy husband's temper will be good, and he will make thee happy, if thou dost not attempt to rule over him.

Were thou chaste as ice, and pure as snow, thou canst not escape slander.

As the frail bark is tossed on the ocean, so wilt thou be on the stormy sea of life; but in the end thou shalt enter the haven of prosperity.

It signifieth that thou must take heed to avoid danger.

Unlooked-for fortune and happiness await thee.

Teach not thy children to be avaricious, and they will be both contented and happy.

Marriage, when prudently undertaken, is the happiest state into which man can enter.

Fear not that the darling of thy heart may prove inconstant.

He will not tarry long.

A nation accustomed to changes hath still to undergo a great one.

Blame not thy servant unjustly.

Friends are so scarce, that, when found, they are to be valued above all price.

What brooks fame, if thou hast no fortune?

As the drooping plant is refreshed by the dew of heaven, so will thy heart be gladdened by sudden prosperity.

Divide thy inheritance with those who have an equal right with thyself.

Y

Rely not too much on present good fortune.

Use no servile means to procure favour; thou shalt be exalted without their aid.

The eye of a master is worth his two hands.

Avoid everything that savours of hell.

Thy expectations from the law are vain; thou shalt not succeed.

Await thy happy destiny at home.

It is utter vanity in thee to desire long life, if thy daily habits tend to destroy it.

Cherish and support the poor captive, who will soon be unfettered.

Content will render this union a complete paradise.

Thou shalt be blessed with sons and daughters; but forget not that they may follow in your footsteps.

A slight disorder affecteth the person concerning whom thou art solicitous, but it will soon pass away.

The barbed arrow which shall be shot at thee by secret enemy, will recoil on his own head.

If thou likest cabbage, use the needle.

Treasures are but rarely found; throw not thy time away in searching after them.

Comport thyself to the customs of those whom thous meetest on thy journey, and thou shalt meet with little annoyance.

Thou shalt in time attain to greater happiness in this matter, than thou canst at present venture to hope for.

Z

There is much harmony in the love which thou and the darling of thy heart bear to each other.

The patient will assuredly recover from the present illness.

Thy husband will be rich; but his constant aim will be to bear sway over thee, and to keep thee under.

The evil reports of thine enemies will not affect thy character.

Few difficulties await thee.

The interpretation is: that if thou observest any blemish in thine own conduct, that thou shouldest lose no time in correcting it.

Shrink not from encountering whatever may occur to thee :– what thou now deemest misfortune may ultimately turn to thy advantage.

Instil honour and honesty into the minds of thy children, and fear not for their prosperity and happiness.

Let no one interfere in the domestic feuds of married persons:– if left alone they will soon subside, and the parties will be happy as before.

Forget not to keep up written communication with the beloved of thy heart.

Let preparations be made for his speedy return from abroad.

Where insolent oppression reigns, where tears water the soil, and where sighs fan the scanty harvest, the freed husbandman will sit under his fig-tree, reveling in the joys of abundance.

Accuse not the innocent rashly.

If thou art joined in pact with another to act wickedly, expect not that he will prove faithful to thee.

The applauses of the wicked are unprofitable, but the praises of the just are like honey which droppeth from the comb.

Correct those faults in thyself which thou seest in others, and thou shalt be happy.

Z

The legacy that will be bequeathed unto thee, will not much profit thee, if thou spendest it foolishly.

Lose not thy all by rash speculation.

Be not servile in adversity, nor despotic in thy prosperity.

Yea! If thou dost steadily avoid immoral haunts.

Better even sleep away thy time, than spend it in ruining thyself or others.

Endeavour to settle all differences in a private manner.

Venture thyself on the ocean without fear.

The wicked old man is a very wretch, who tastes of hell before his time. Wouldest thou be aged and wicked too? Go to! Rather let the sapling wither than the tree be rotten.

Visit the captive who is in affliction; but his woes will soon be turned into joys.

Thou shalt marry a very worthy personage, who will inherit considerable property.

As the protecting oak is encircled by the tender ivy, so shall a numerous race of sons and daughters claim thy paternal regard.

Thy friend is in good health at the present time; he is in the act of bestowing charity.

Act with caution, and thou shalt undoubtedly triumph over a powerful enemy.

Obtain an insight into two trades in which the hands are principally employed; reflect on both for a week, and follow that of which thou dreamest.

Be as industrious as thou art now covetous, and great riches will be thy reward.

Be not affected by the petty inconveniences which thou mayest meet with; else, if thou shouldest be beset with real dangers, thou shalt not have courage to face them.

Go well armed and accoutred, and dispute not with thy companions on the way, and thy journey will be safe and prosperous.

Thy image is ever before the eyes of thy beloved.

The patient's disorder will yield to proper remedies.

Thou shalt be united to a man whose complexion is dark, but whose features are handsome.

The evil report of thine enemies will recoil on their own heads.

Prosperity will succeed misfortune.

It signifieth that thy conduct requireth amendment.

Fear not that thy misfortunes will continue to pursue thee.

Those concerning whom thou art anxious, are prosperous and happy.

Let each concede to the other in matters of trifling import, and both will be happy.

Give thy beloved no cause to prove inconstant to thee.

He must still remain a stranger for a brief season.

The air which has long been filled with the sighs of oppression, will soon resound with the shouts of "Liberty."

Be secret, and examine each person singly.

If thou expectest that a companion in wickedness will prove a faithful friend, thou art deceived.

Enter upon no design of which thou hast not well considered whether it will reflect on thy honour.

Napoleon's Oracle

Avoid the snares of thine enemies.

Although thou inheritest property, still be industrious and frugal.

If thou hast enough of earthly goods, therewith be content, and run no risks.

Interest will procure thee great favour from others.

Avoid cards, women and wine – and prosper.

Thy risks are great, thy chance of gaining small – and in the end, perhaps, thou wilt lose thy all.

The gain at best will be trivial.

Be steady in thy resolution to turn thy back on thy native shores.

So bear thyself toward thy children and thy kinsfolk that they may watch over and protect thee when age weareth thee down, and thy powers fail thee.

The captive will be released, but let him beware of again falling into the clutches of power.

Thou shalt have an honourable, young and handsome partner.

Sons will be born unto thee :– train them in their youth in the way they should go, and when they are old they will not depart from it.

Thy friend is in the enjoyment of good health, but is not entirely divested of cares.

See that thy conduct be such that men may love and not hate thee.

Choose a business in which the hands rather than the head are employed.

When thou findest a treasure, teach thy tongue to be silent, and see that thou makest good use of thy riches.

If thou diggest up thy fields with the plough of industry, thou wilt find a treasure which will reward thee.

Thy journey will be prosperous.

Thou mayest hope to get a place in the affections of the darling of thy soul.

The pain with which the patient is afflicted, will soon be terminated.

Thy husband will be exalted to a high station.

Thy slanderers are busy, but they will be baffled in their endeavours to injure thee.

Great difficulties await thee; but they will not much affect thy future fortune.

The signification is that good luck will befall thee.

Misfortunes may be thy lot in the beginning, but in the end will be peace and happiness.

Fail not duly to instruct thy children in all knowledge which may be meet for them, and they will assuredly profit in the end.

Mutual forbearance is the strongest bond of matrimonial felicity.

The affections of the being whom thou lovest will be placed on none other but thyself.

He will come back with abundance of riches and knowledge.

He who ruleth the kings of the earth, and who terrifieth the nations with the sound of his arms, be abased and speedily cut off.

Be sure of thy grounds before thou enterest on a prosecution.

Choose thy friends only from among the virtuous, and fear no treachery.

The approval of thy Creator is more profitable than the empty applauses of men.

Be select in the choice of thy friends, and the future will be happier than the past.

Thou, thou inheritest houses and lands, what availeth if thou art not prudent?

Impediments will start up which thou dreamest not of.

Be honourable and honest in thy dealings, and thou shalt be greatly exalted.

Thou wilt find the benefit of neither giving nor taking long credits.

Leave off play as the clock strikes twelve; after that hour there is no luck for thee.

Expectest thou to snatch the burning oil from the devouring flames? No more think of rescuing thy goods out of the fire of the law, if once it feedeth on them.

Thou shalt visit distant regions where gold aboundeth – in thy prosperity, forget not the widow and orphan.

It is not meet for thee to desire old age, if thou dost too freely indulge thy carnal appetite.

Captivity, anxiety, suspense, liberty and joy, will rapidly succeed each other.

Thou shalt marry thy equal in worth and fortune: be content and happy.

As the roses bloom upon the parent tree, so will sons and daughters grace thee by their beauty.

The objects of thy anxious inquiries are well; they are equally solicitous about thy welfare.

Thou wilt be envied; but it should be thy constant care that even thine enemies shall have cause to admire thy virtues.

Choose not a business which depends on the luxury and whim of the age in which thou livest.

Often men in low circumstances have risen by their industry to the loftiest stations. Go thou and do likewise.

Lose no time from thy business in looking after hidden treasures.

Prosperity will attend thy travels, but thou must still be prudent.

Rejoice! Thou art truly beloved.

The patient's disorder will soon be greatly alleviated.

Thy husband will possess great riches.

Let thy reputation be founded in virtue, and thou needest not dread the rancorous shafts of slander.

Fear not that fortune will desert thee.

It importeth kindness and charity to thy poor friends.

After rain cometh sunshine.

As thou hopest happiness for thy children, lead them in the paths of virtue and honour.

Misfortunes may becloud the dawn of matrimony, but the evening will be serene and happy.

Doubt not the vows of love which have been made to thee.

A certain circumstance prevents his immediate return.

Those who have long sighed for freedom shall soon attain it

When thou hast discovered the thief, see that his punishment be proportioned to his crime.

NAPOLEON'S ORACLE

If thou expectest thy friend to be true, be true to him.

If thy deeds are just, fear not but that future generations will hold thy memory in esteem.

A man's happiness depends entirely upon the company which he keeps.

O man! Forget not that the goods which thou inheritest are not of thine own earning; therefore remember the poor in the days of thy prosperity.

Before thou buildest, reckon the cost of thy house.

Thy fame will be exalted above thy fellows.

Rise early, mind thy business, be regular in thy accounts, and prosper.

Never drink until the game is ended.

Verily it will be vanity in thee to expect success in thy suit.

Fortune will favour thee in thine own country.

Longevity and sensual gratification are incompatible :– think not of enjoying both.

The captive will at length escape, and triumph over his enemies.

You will marry a person with whom you will have much comfort.

Thou shalt have three lovely daughters; instruct and watch over them as thou wouldest over the apple of thine eye.

Thy friend enjoyeth health and happiness; he is in the act of counting money.

Heed not the feeble and impotent attempts of him who will attempt to do thee injury.

||

Thou hast enemies, who, if not restrained by fear of the law, would plunge a dagger in thy heart.

The soldier's bayonet hath sometimes given place to the field-marshal's baton.

The treasure thou wilt find will be a partner whose affectionate heart will share thy happiness and sympathize in all thy sorrows.

No ill-luck will befall thee.

There is no lack of regard on the part of thy beloved.

The patient's illness will yield to proper remedies.

Thou shalt wed a man of much substance.

Thou shalt be well spoken of.

Be prudent and thy difficulties will bring thee nearer to the happiness destined for thee.

It portendeth danger if thou art not cautious.

The clouds on thy brow will be dispersed by beams of fortune and happiness.

Restrain thy children when they indulge in wicked courses, and when they become fathers, they will have cause to bless thy name.

Fear not that misfortune will attend this marriage.

Thine own fidelity and that of thy beloved, will be rewarded with happiness.

The stranger will return but not speedily.

Tyranny will soon be engulfed in the abyss of its new iniquity.

||

By perseverance only shalt thou recover thy goods.

When thou askest advice of thy friend, relate not to him thy story by halves, lest in concealing the matter from him thou suffer in the end.

In future ages shall thy name be cited as a pattern for rising generations, if thou art the benefactor of mankind.

Avoid the haunts of the wicked and be happy.

Thine own earnings will prove much sweeter than the largest inheritance.

Be exceedingly cautious in thy present speculations.

Be true to thy present trust, and thou shalt have affairs of much importance committed to thy care.

The industrious man is seldom the fortunate one.

Confine thyself to games, wherein thou mayest overcome thy rival by ingenuity and fair play.

Thou wilt soon obtain what thou little expectest.

If thou goest far abroad, thy kinsmen at home will not deal justly by thee :– tarry not by the way.

Old age never commands respect, unless it be allied with virtue :– wouldest thou be old and detested too?

The captive will live to see his enemies punished.

Thy partner will, if used well, go through every danger for thee.

As the parent trunk giveth up a part of its nourishment to the tender shoots which spring from its sides, so will sons and daughters require thy succour and protection.

Fear not for the health of thy friends; they are in expectation that thou wilt send them some small matter whereby they may keep thee in remembrance.

Thy friends are well, and sleep soundly in the mansion of content and happiness.

Thy enemies will not have power to harm thee.

Make a bold effort to let all men hear your message.

It will not be thy fortune to discover hidden treasures.

Let prudence be thy guide, and thou wilt reach thy journey's end in safety.

The beloved of thy soul adores thee in secret.

Let every means be used for the restoration of health.

The good temper of thy husband will make thee happy.

Waste not thy time by seeking for the good report of every man.

Man that is born of woman is born to trouble, as the sparks fly upward.

It signifieth that thou ought not to trust another with affairs which thou canst manage thyself.

Let not thy misfortunes unman thee; but prepare thyself for happier times.

When a man of good standing passeth on, happiness and prosperity will attend his offspring.

A marriage founded on avarice is seldom a happy one.

Consult thine own heart, whether thou oughtest to have exacted a vow of constancy.

The stranger will return soon.

The wings of the eagle of the north will be clipped and his talons blunted.

It is necessary for thee to bear thy loss with fortitude.

One act of disinterested friendship should cancel the remembrance of a thousand foibles.

Abuse not the power which the Lord giveth thee, and thy name will be hailed with rapture in future ages.

Thy misfortunes will soon terminate.

Fear not: thine own industry will procure thee a sufficient provision.

Let prudence and justice be thine handmaids, and all thy undertakings will prove successful.

Kick not down the ladder which raises thee up.

A penny saved is a penny got :– a word to the wise is enough.

Effect no mortgage to pay a gambling debt.

Thy hope is vain, justice is blind to thy claims, and fortune shuns thee.

The wealth thou gainest abroad, distribute justly and charitably at home.

To arrive at old age, thou must avoid the causes of premature decay.

Liberty will be proclaimed to the captive.

A handsome, good-natured partner, a bag of gold, and a carriage.

A son will be born unto thee, who will not disappoint the hopes which thou shalt entertain respecting him.

§

Thy wife will bless thee with a large offspring, and will be among them, as the queen of night among the stars of heaven.

Those concerning whom thou art anxious, are well and happy: they now enjoy the sweets of conversation.

Thou hast :– but fear not that they will have power to injure thee.

Write on thy door posts – "Laundry done here!"

The silver and the gold which hath been buried in the earth, will forever be hidden from thy view.

When thou goest forth from thy dwelling, no harm will overtake thee.

Thy love will meet its due return.

Whilst there is life there is hope :– let no means be untried to cure the disorder.

An honourable man will wed thee.

Thy reputation will, in a small degree, be effected by detraction.

Many scenes may be presented before thine eyes.

It importeth that if thou dost procrastinate, evil will attend thee.

Thy misfortunes ought to be thy future monitors:– take heed, and prosperity will attend thee.

To be happy, it is necessary only to be virtuous:– teach this to thy children, and they will be benefitted.

Care not so much for abundance of gold and silver with thy partner as stores of virtue and prudence, and thy marriage will be a happy one.

Lay it not greatly to heart, if the being thou now dotest on should prove changeable.

The stranger's return will be hailed with joy.

The storm of revolution will rage throughout the earth for a time; but in the end, peace and plenty will be diffused among the nations.

When thou hast recovered thy goods, be careful of them for the future.

Let not interested persons have so much power over thee as to cause distrust or discord between thy friend and thee.

Let not thy desire of making thy name live forever urge thee on to deeds of cruelty and rapine.

Happiness and misery are merely relative; therefore make not thyself unhappy for trifles.

Be not intoxicated with good fortune when it arrives.

Rely not on appearances.

Good deeds will prefer thee to honour.

Envy not thy industrious neighbour; but steadily follow his example.

Beware of foul play.

Doth the wolf tamely relinquish his prey, or the fox his booty? How then expectest thou to rescue thy goods from the fangs of the man of law?

Fear not for thy journey – it will be prosperous.

Let temperance be thy nurse and labour thy physician, and thou wilt need none other, for health will be the companion of thy age.

Speedy release for the prisoner.

Your partner will possess houses and lands.

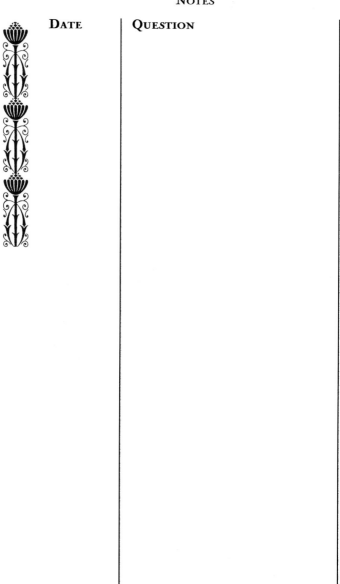

DATE | **QUESTION**

ANSWERS